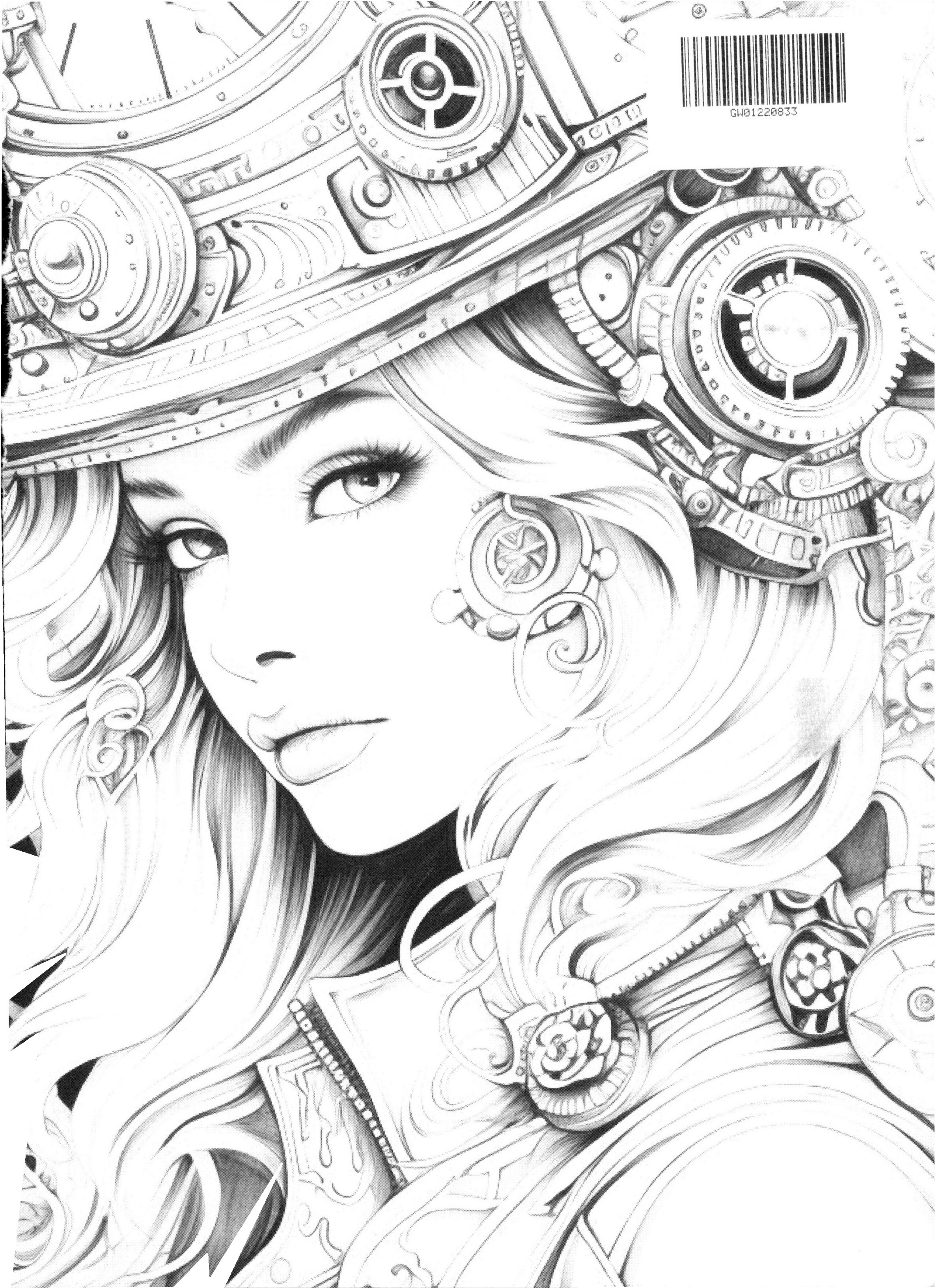

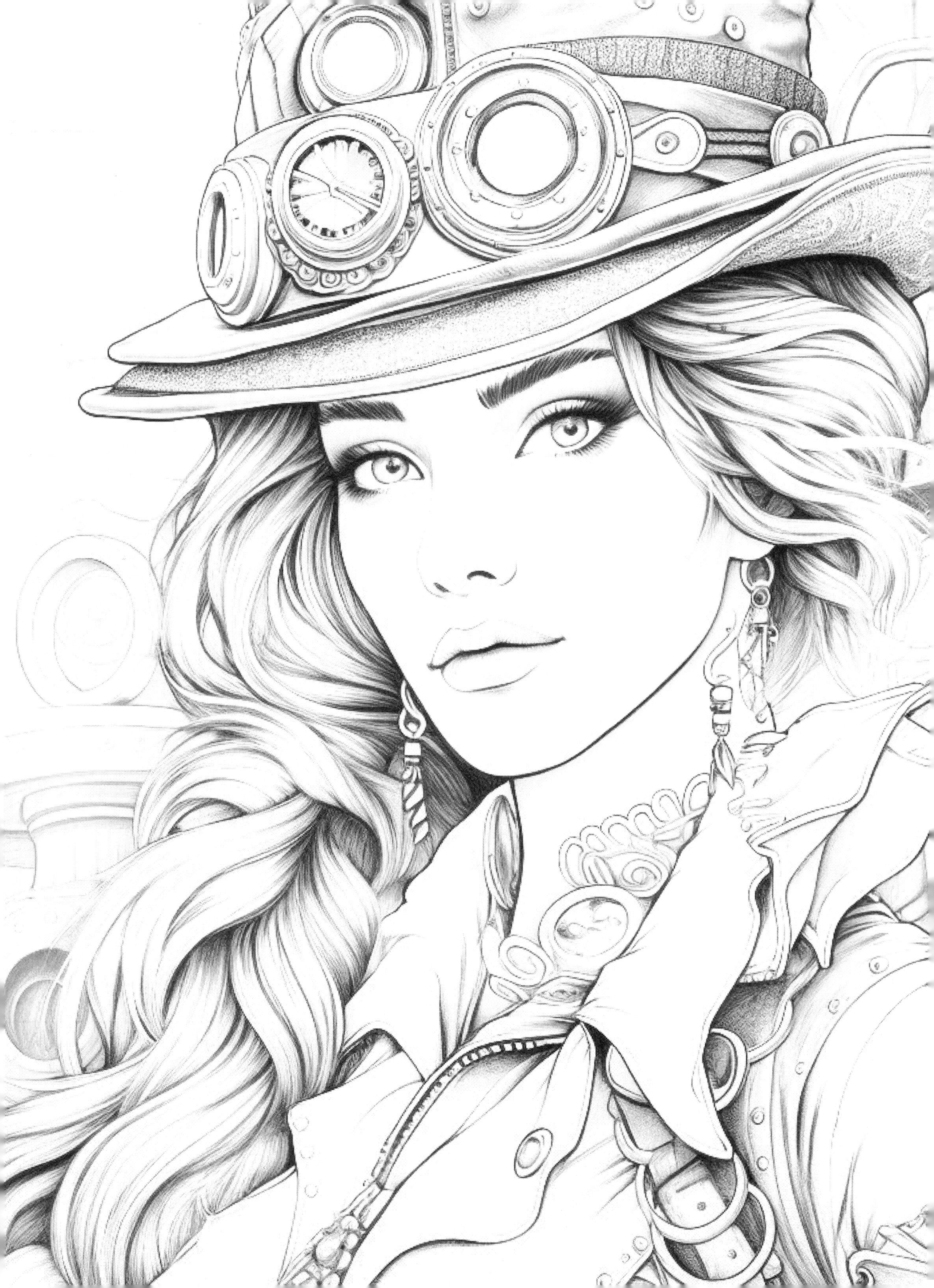

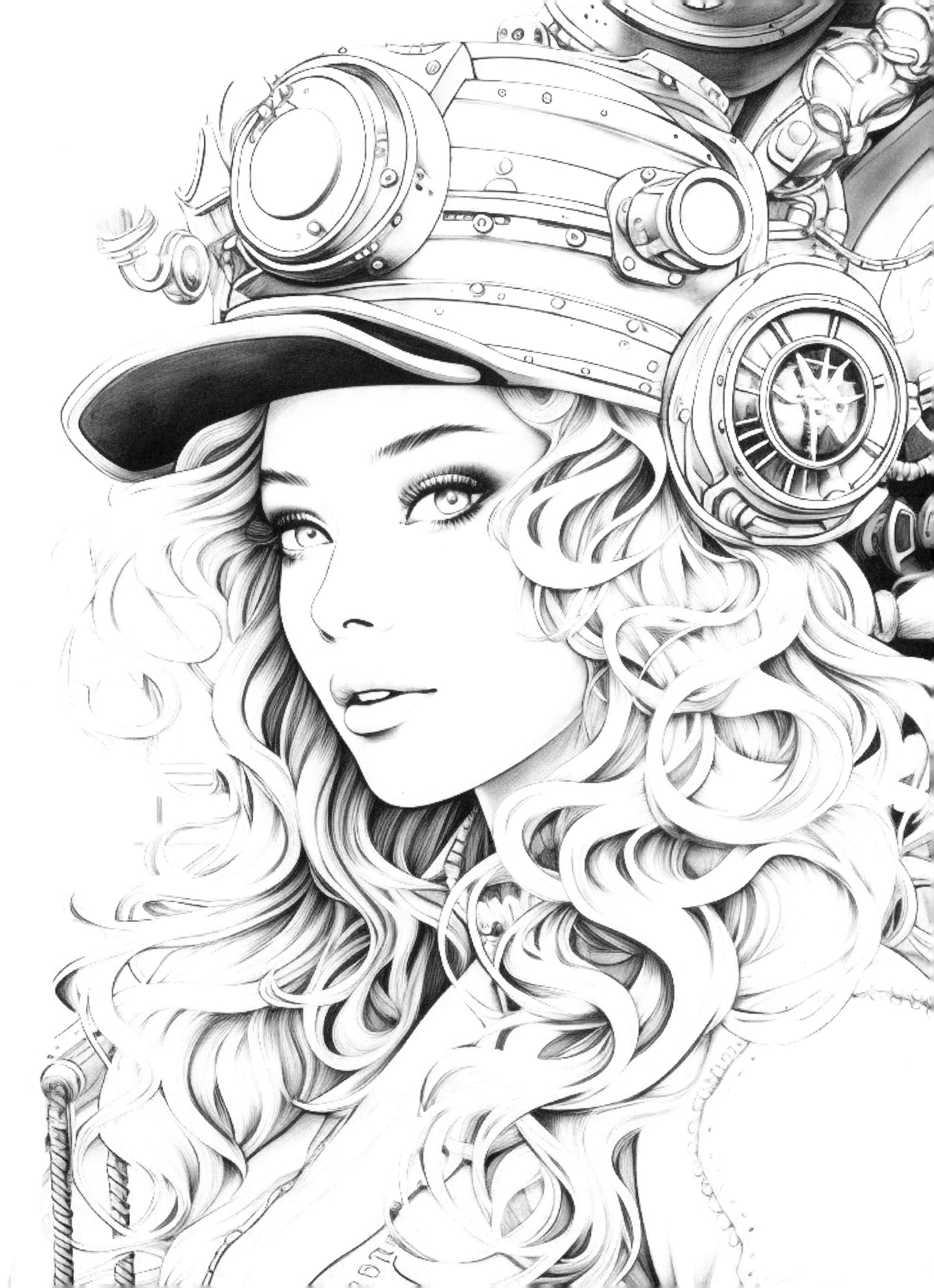

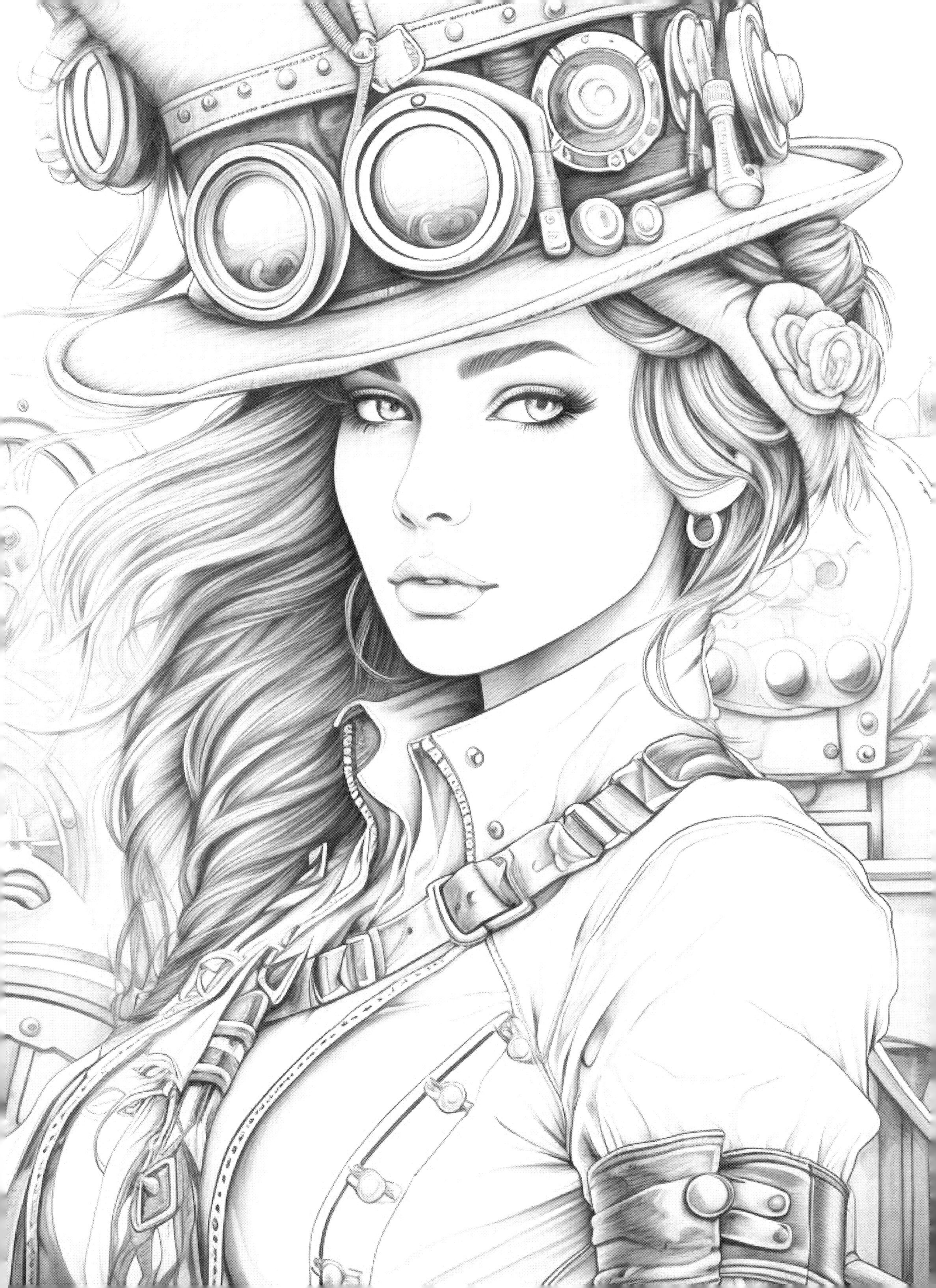

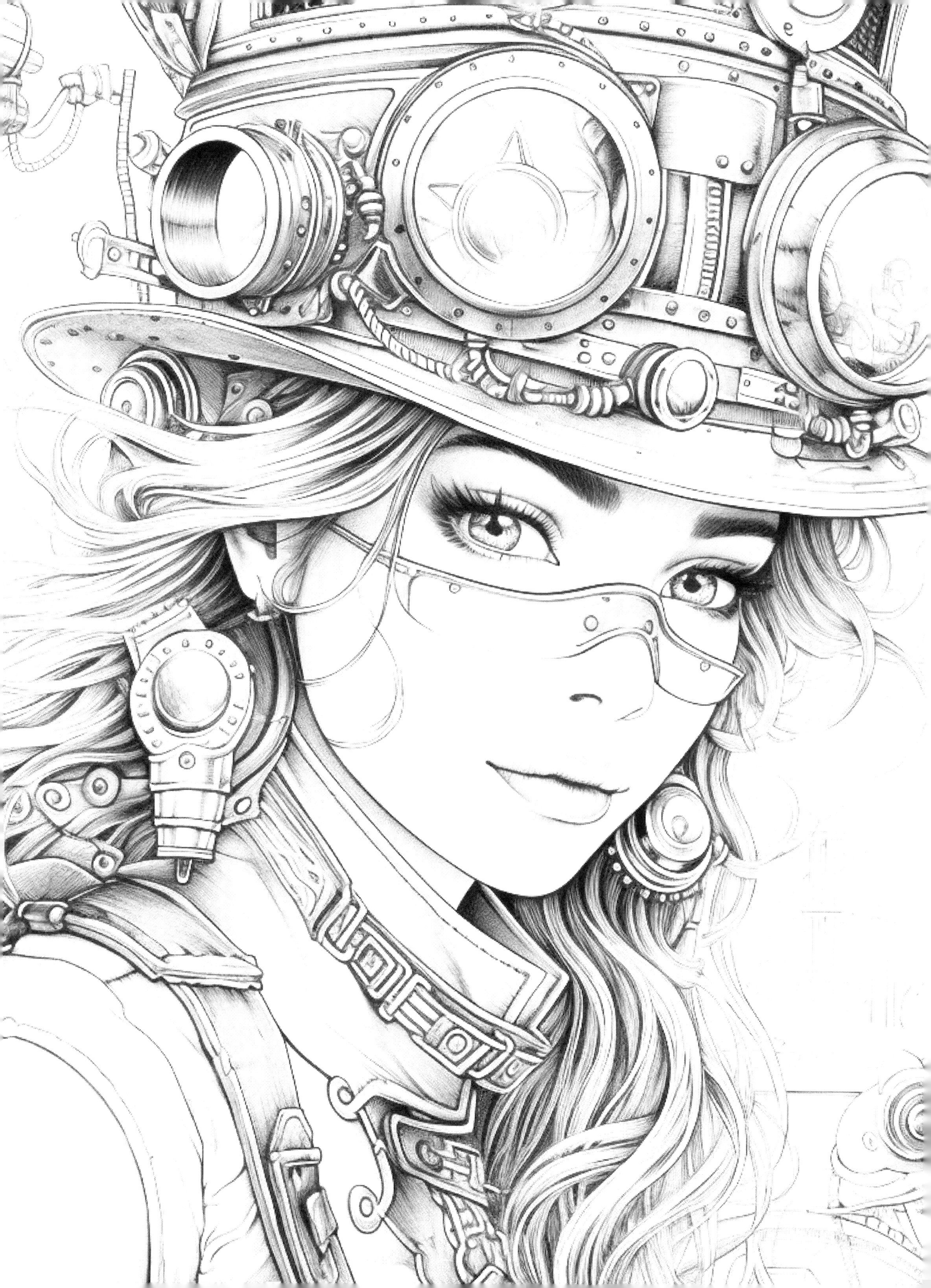

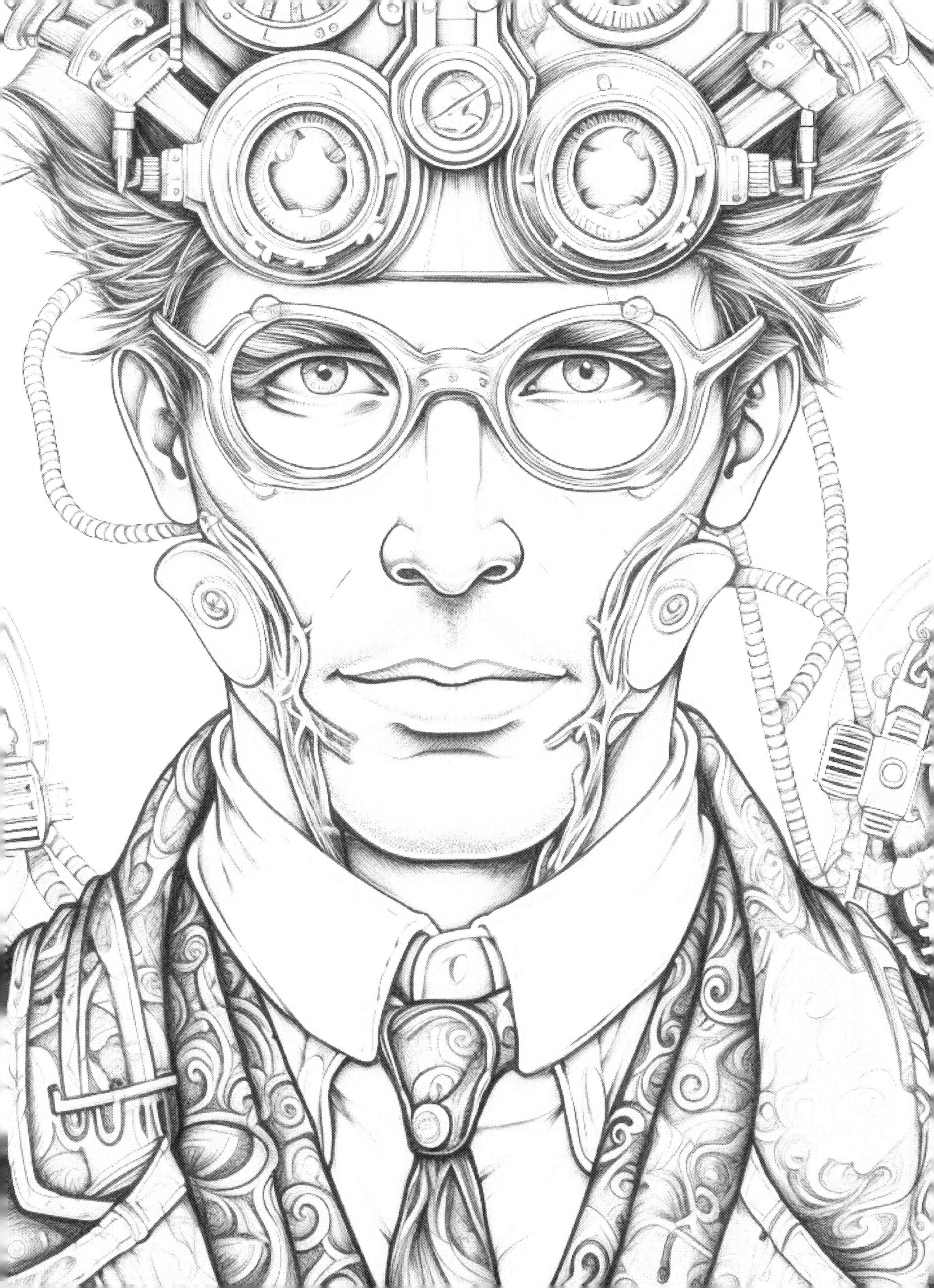

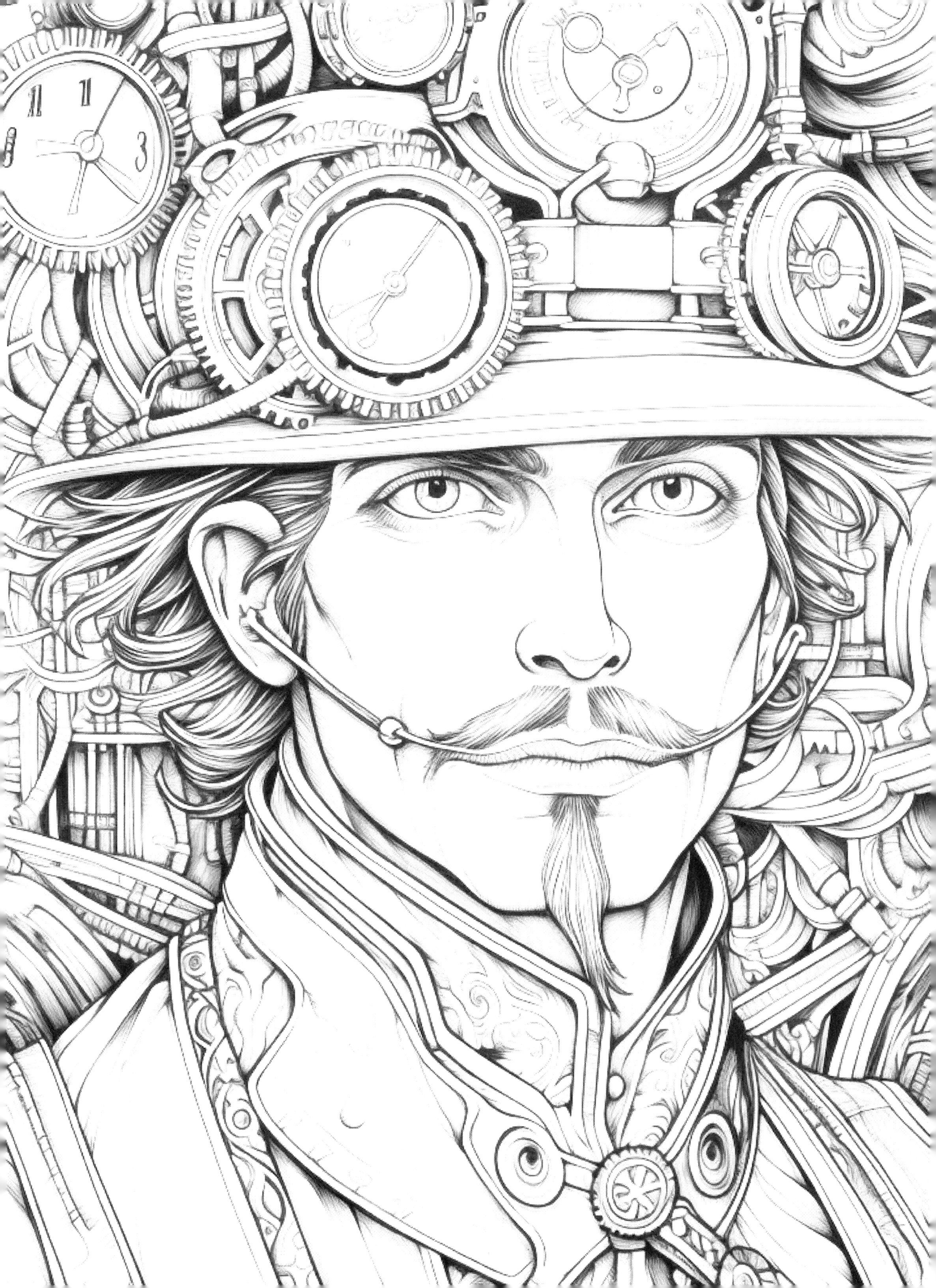

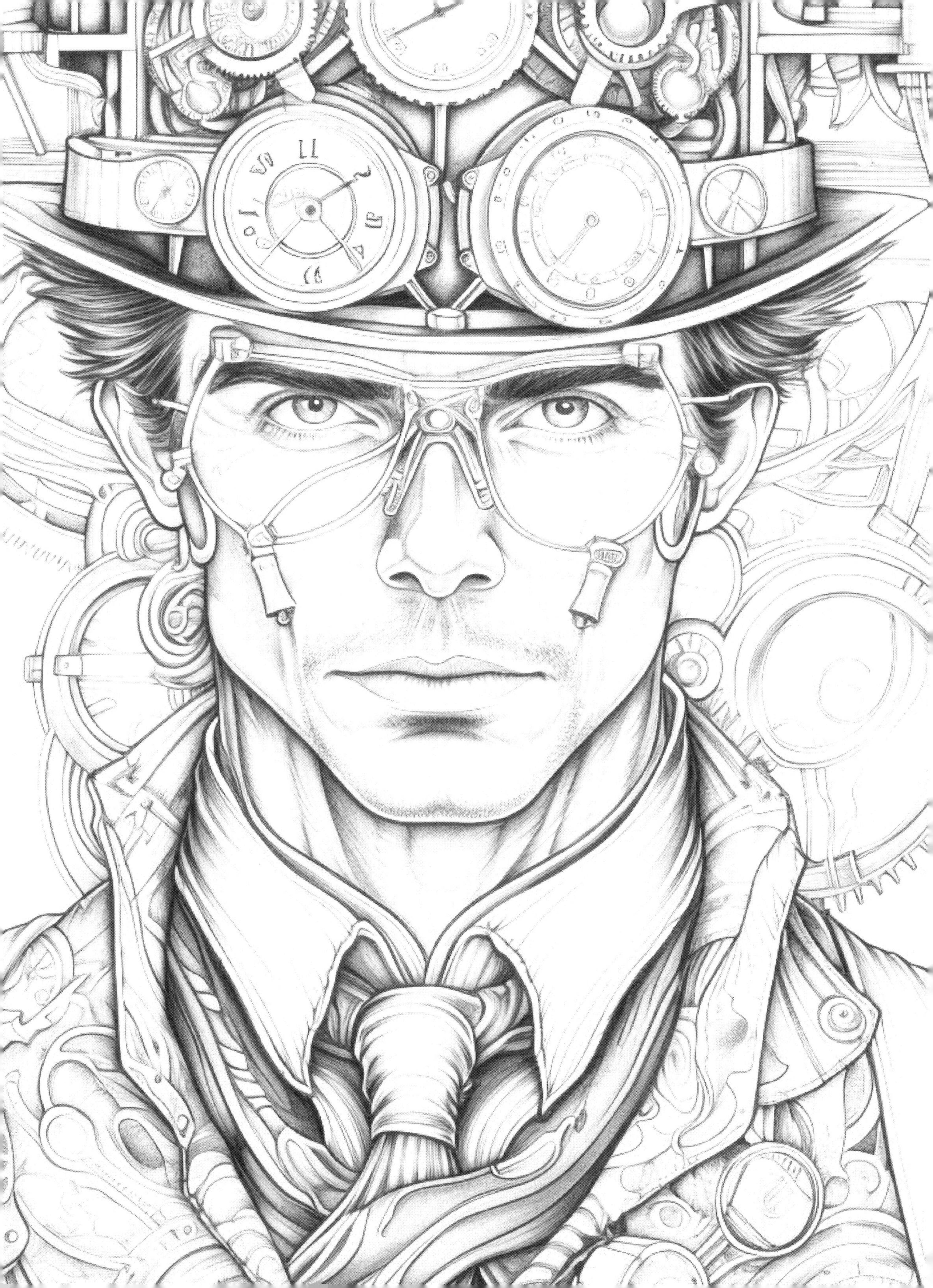

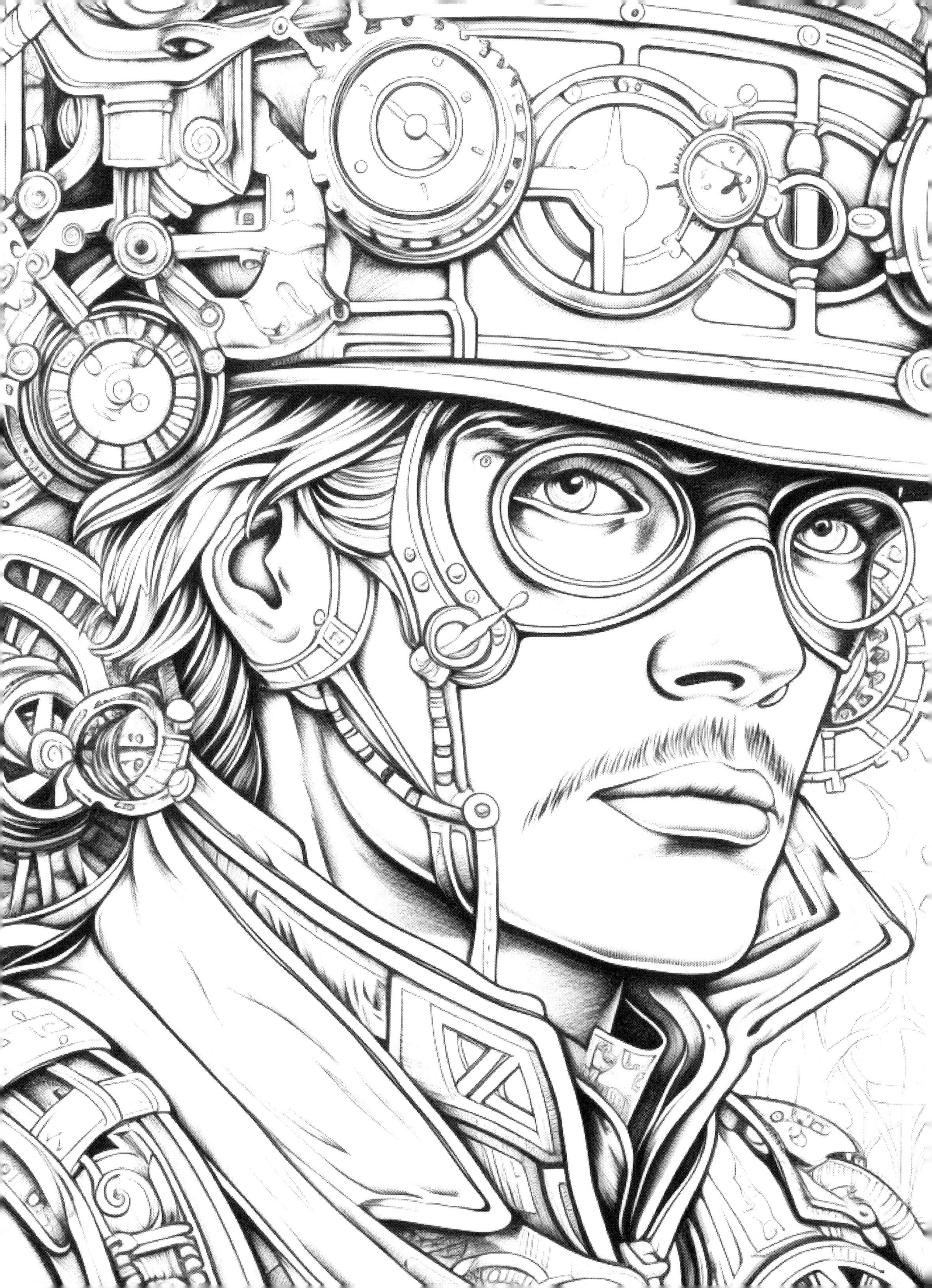

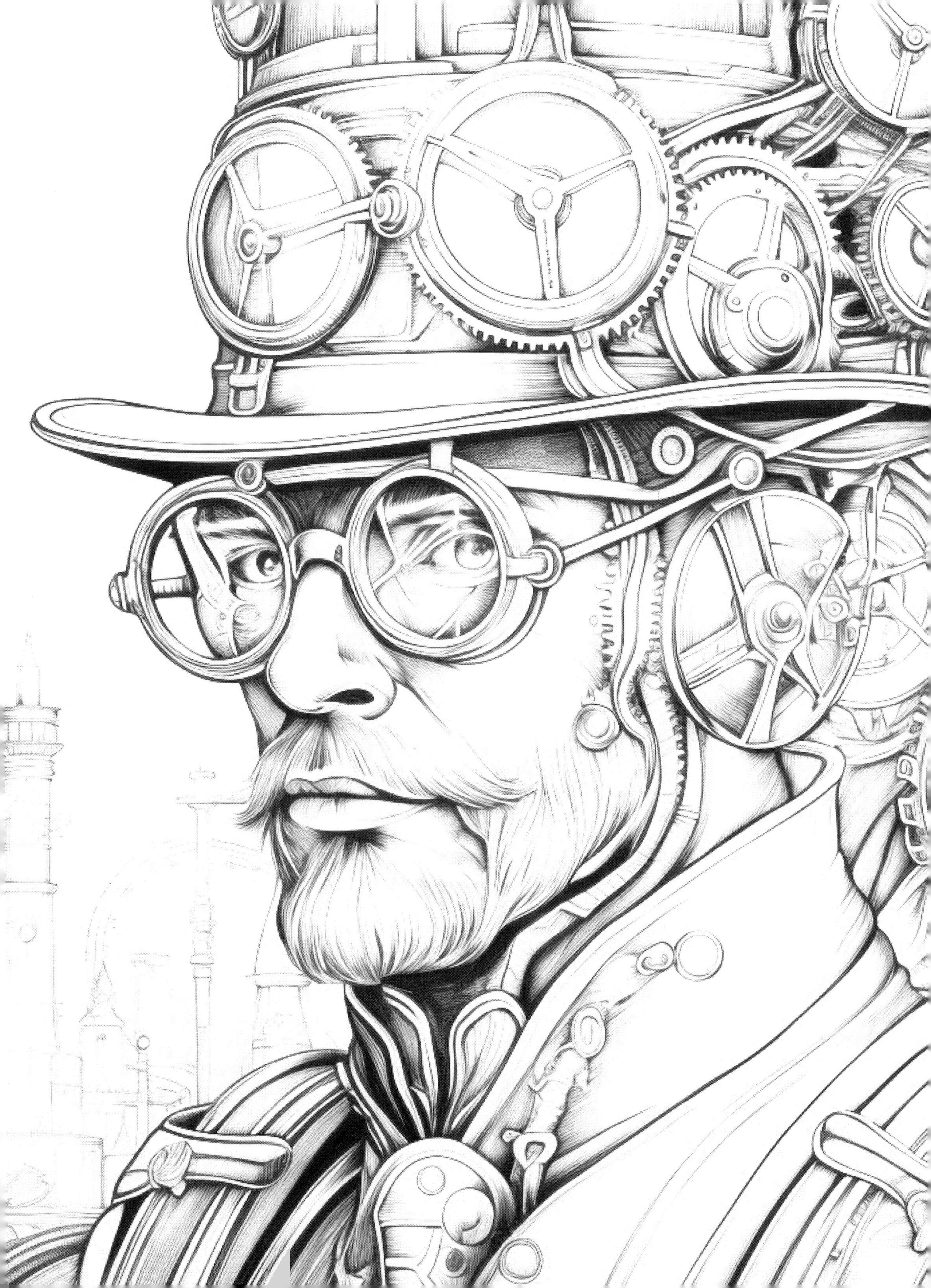

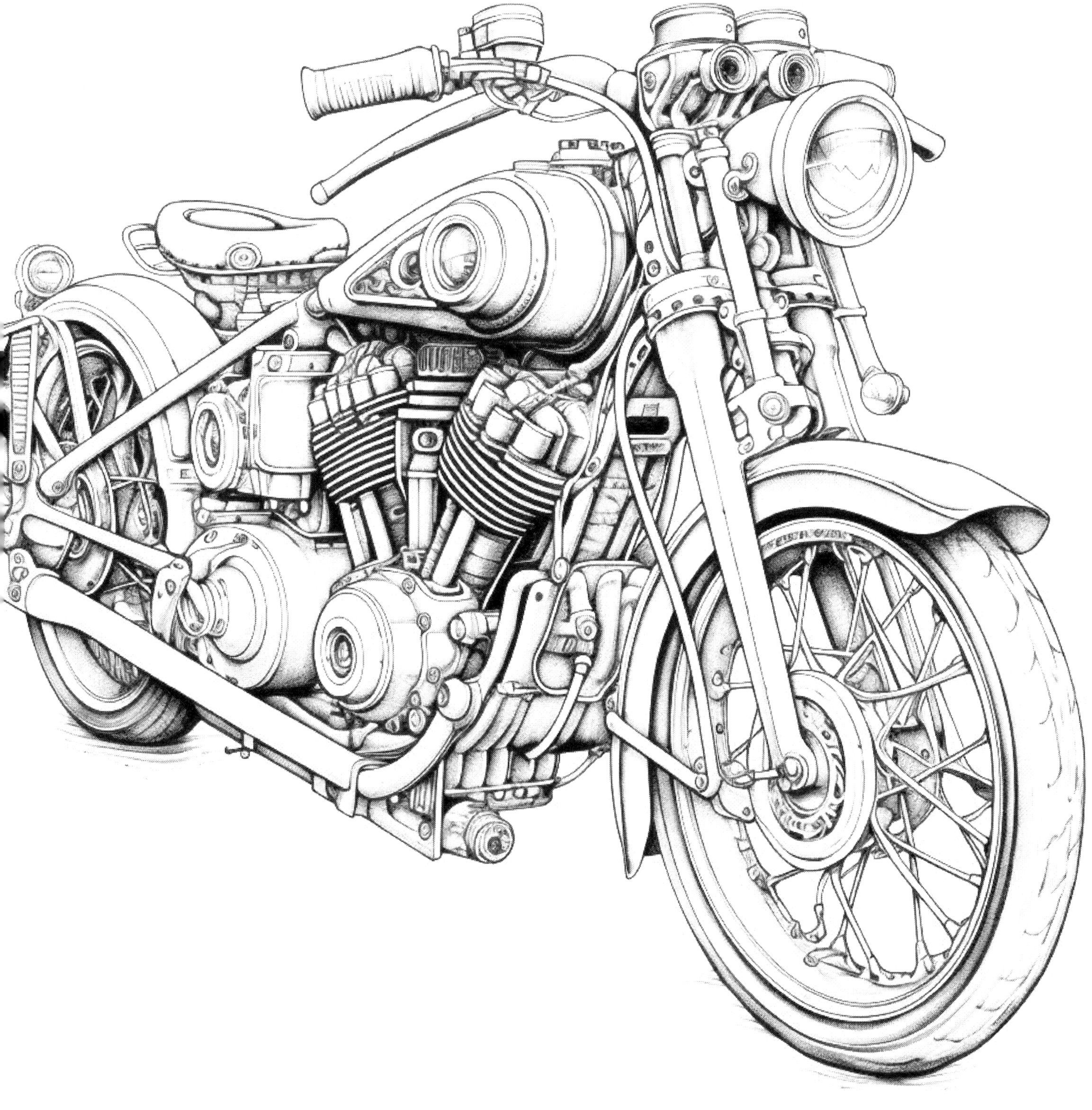

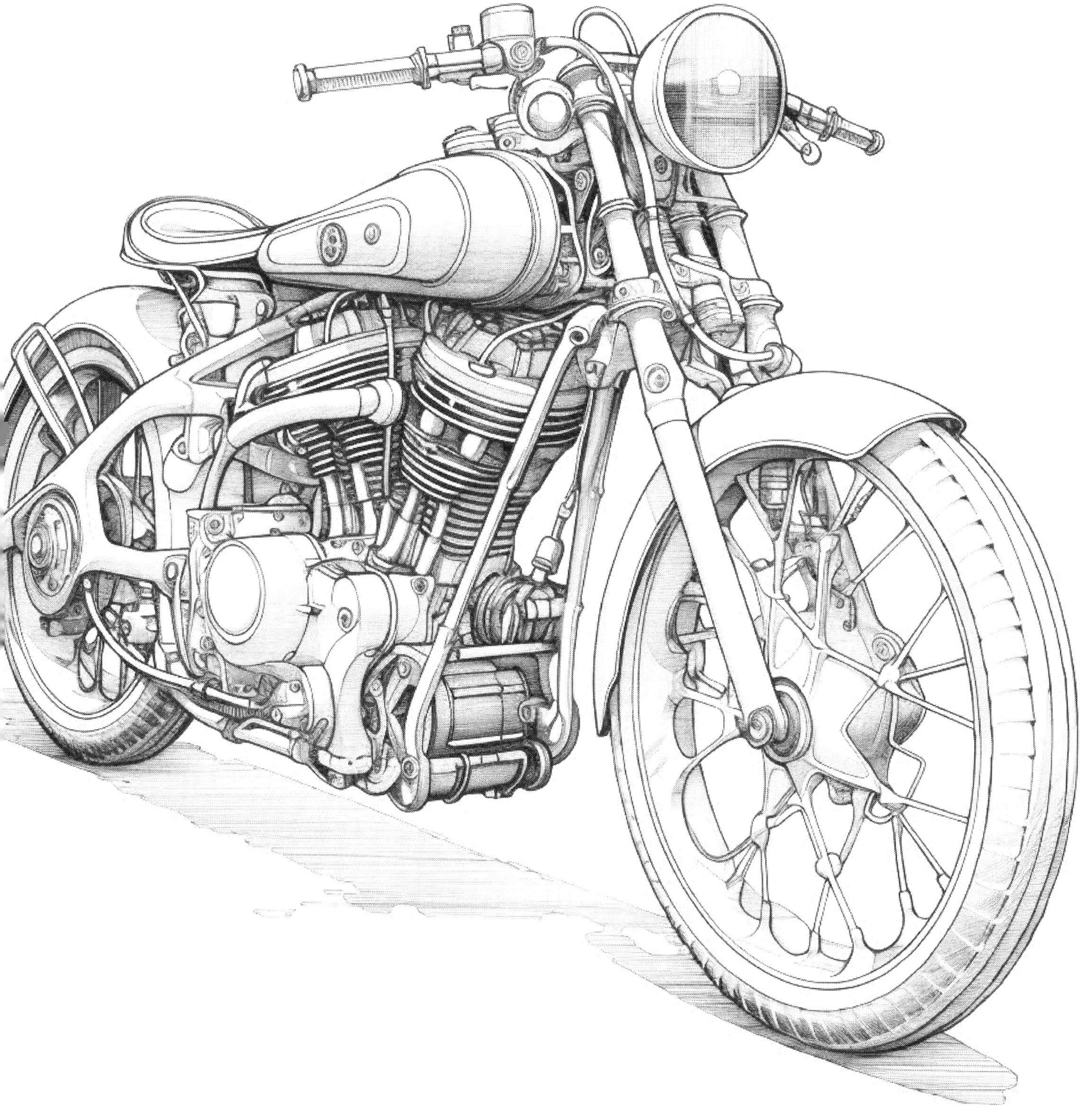

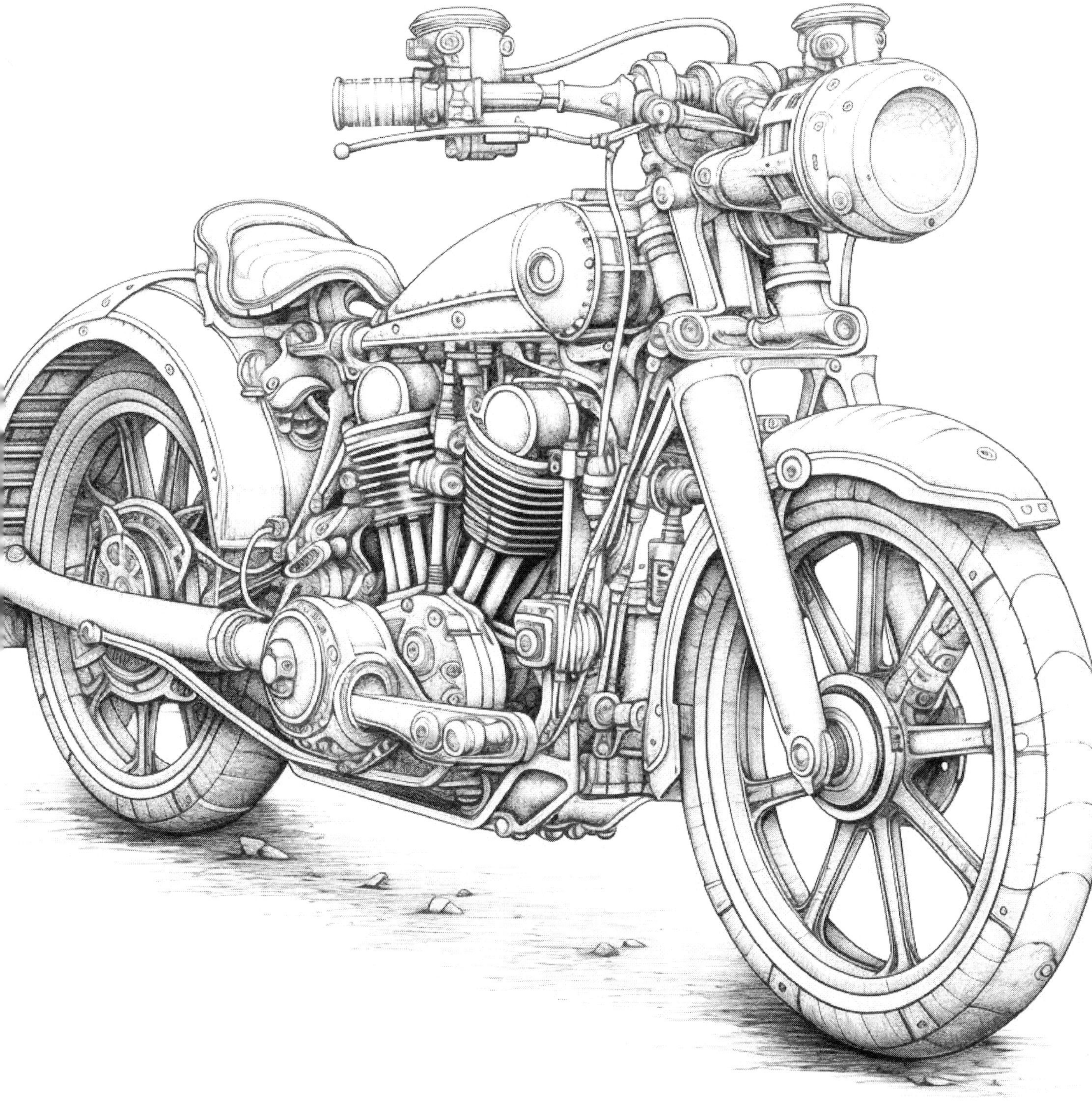

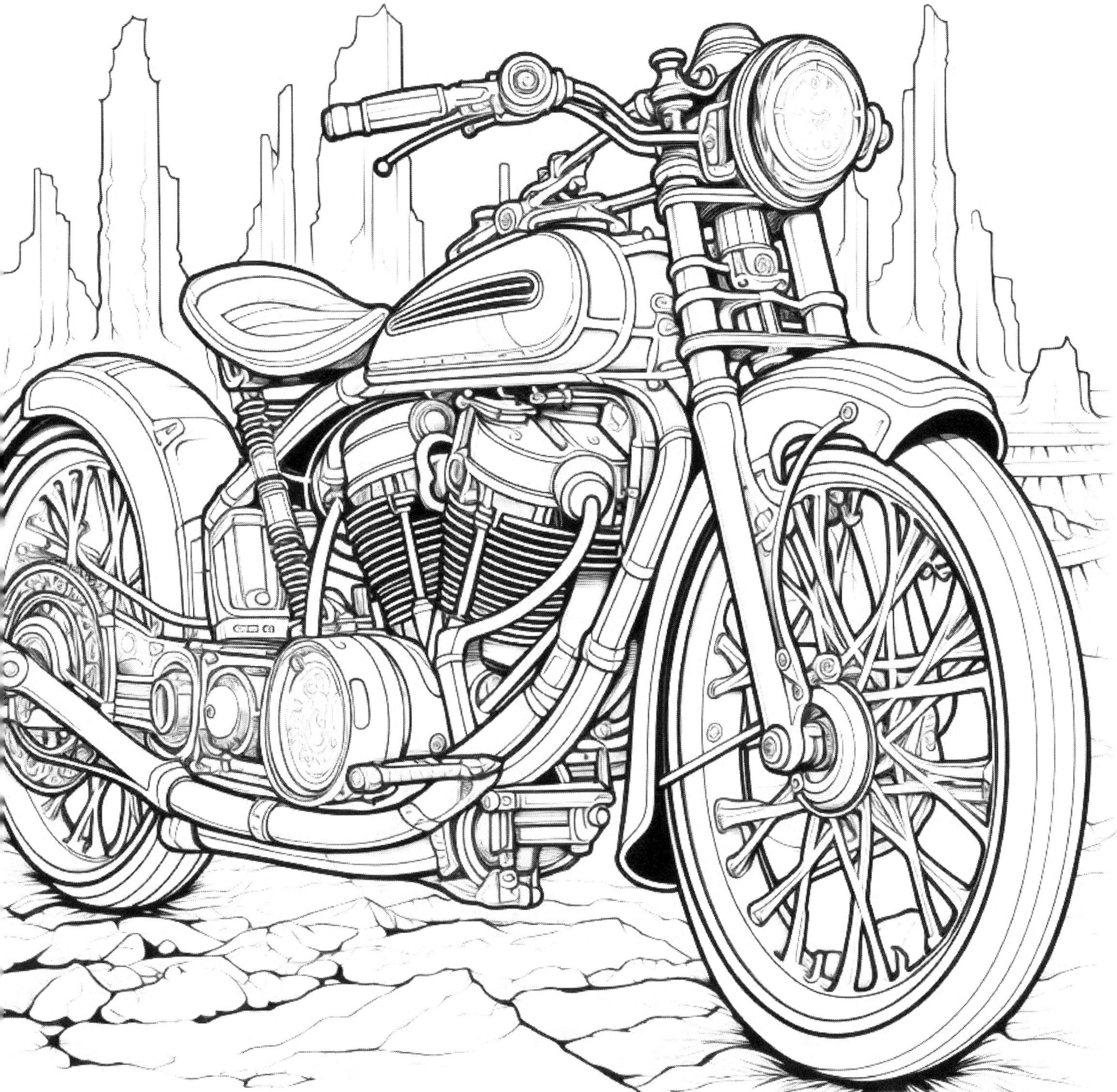

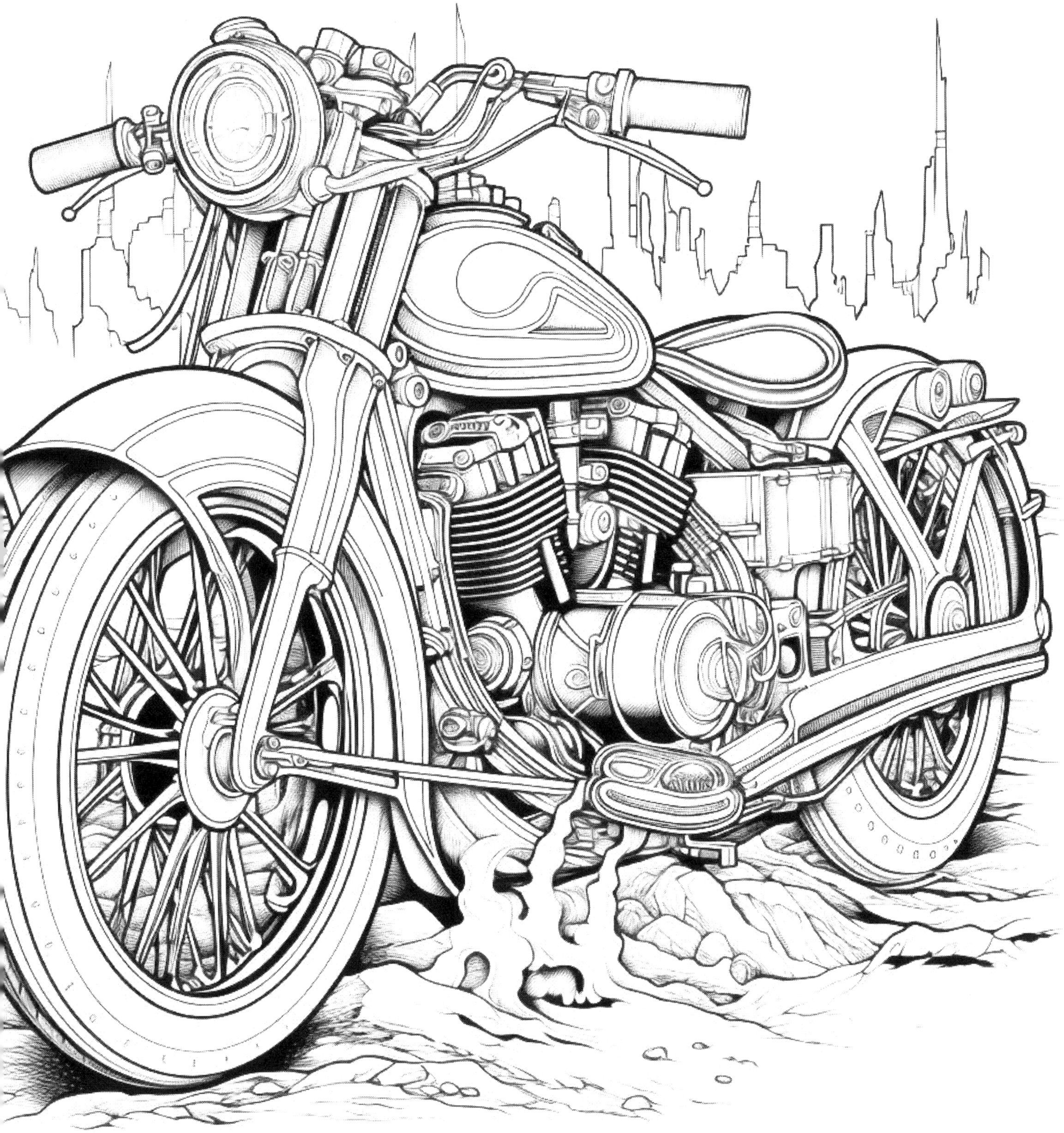

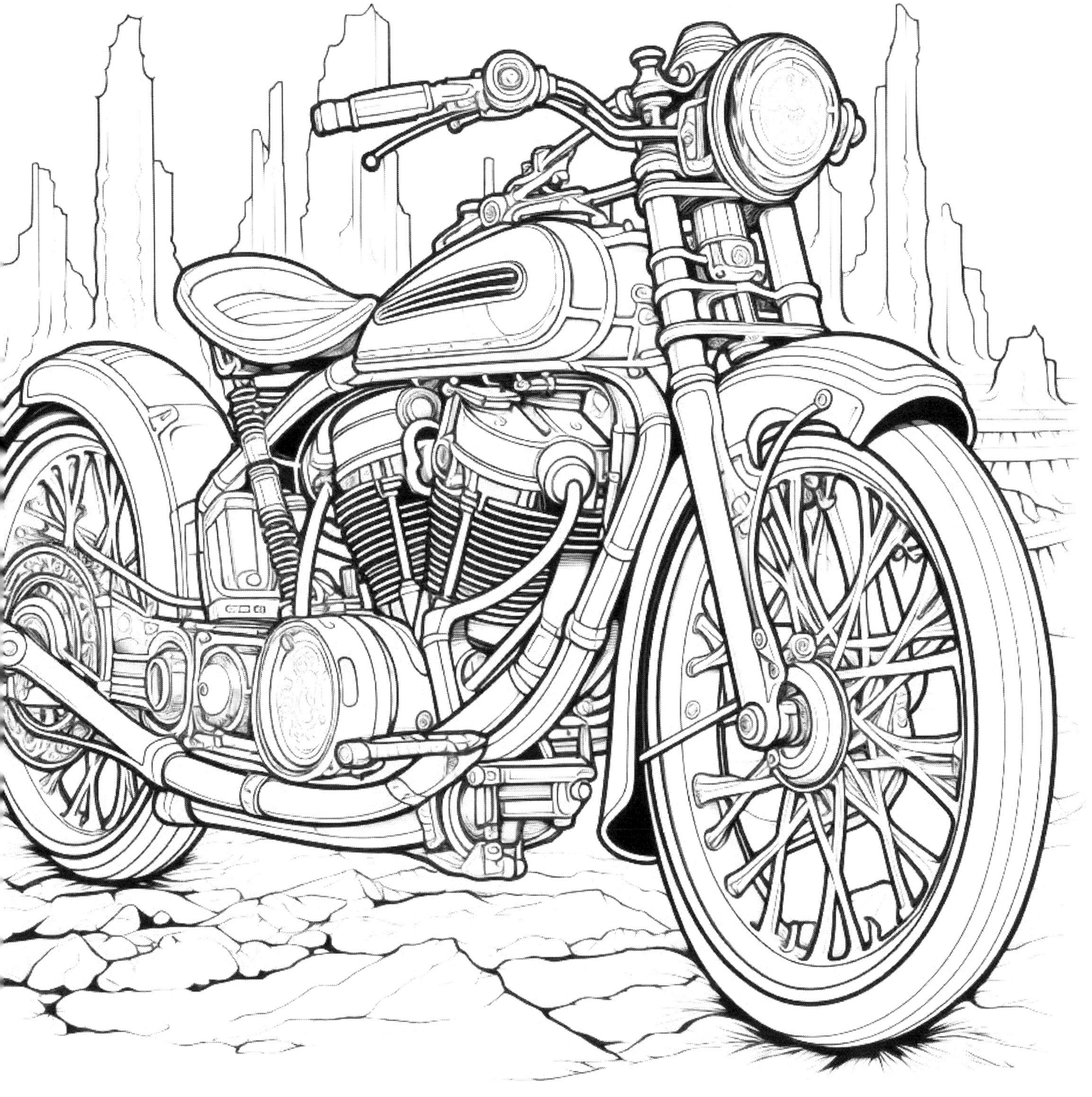

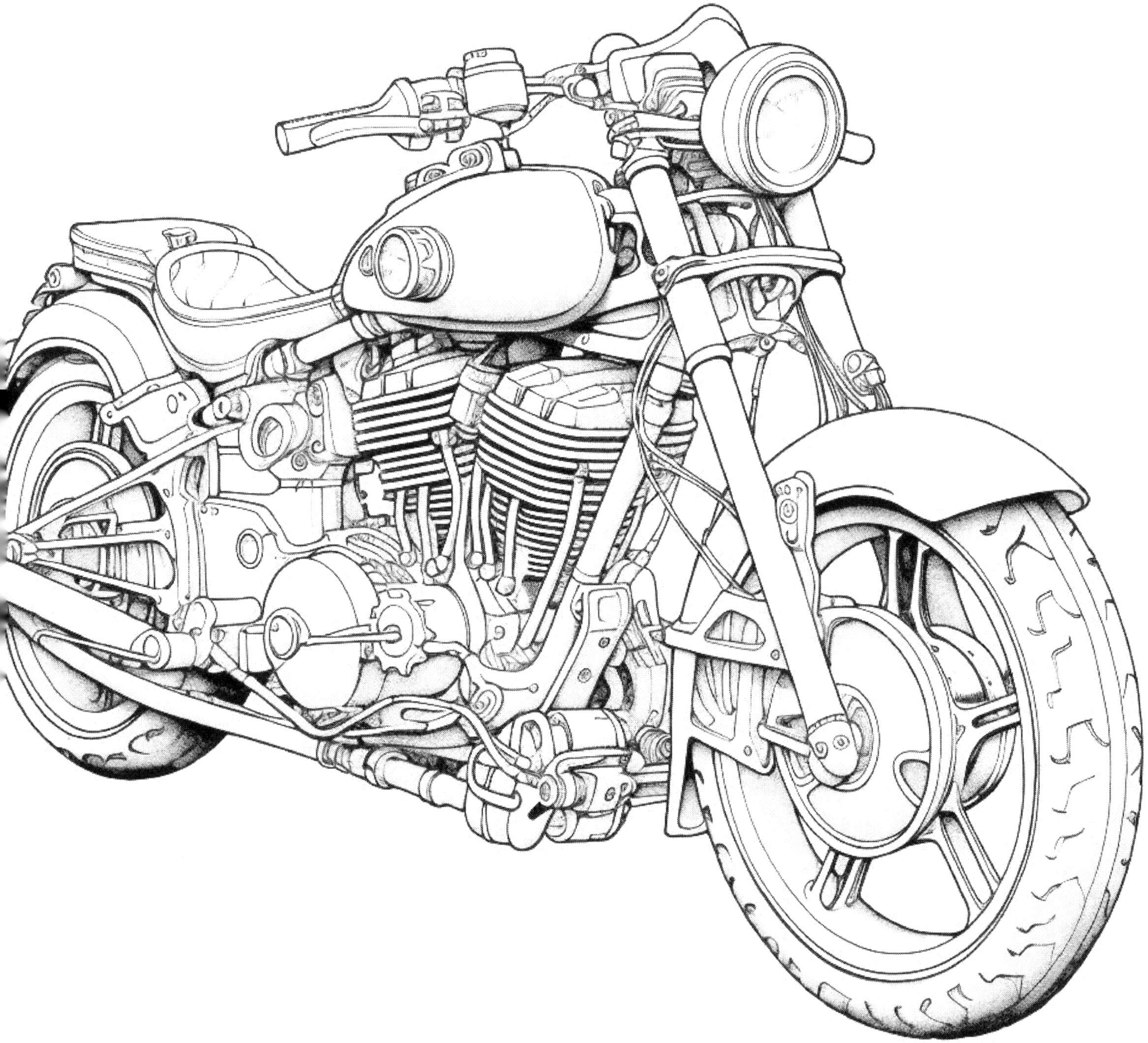

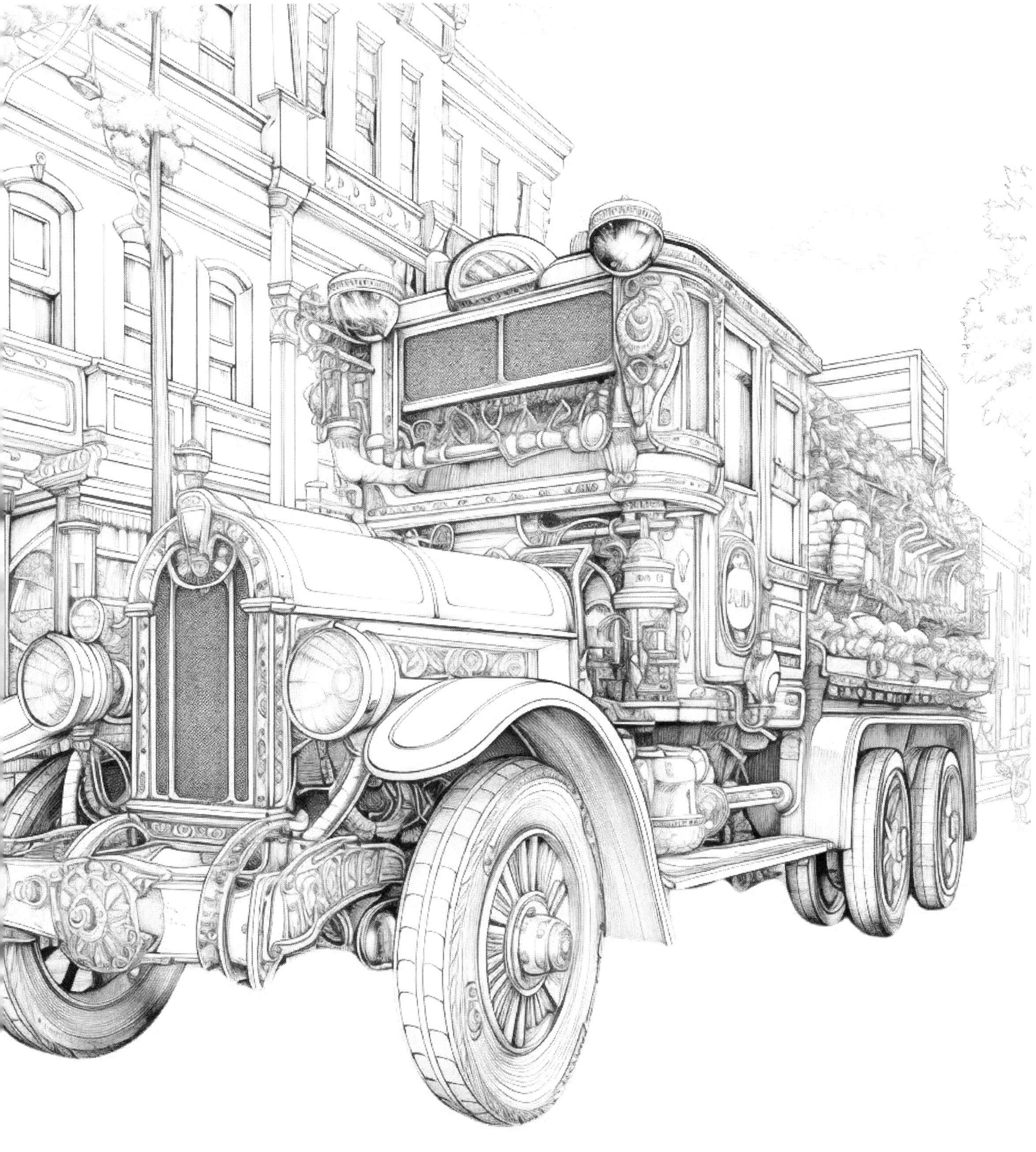

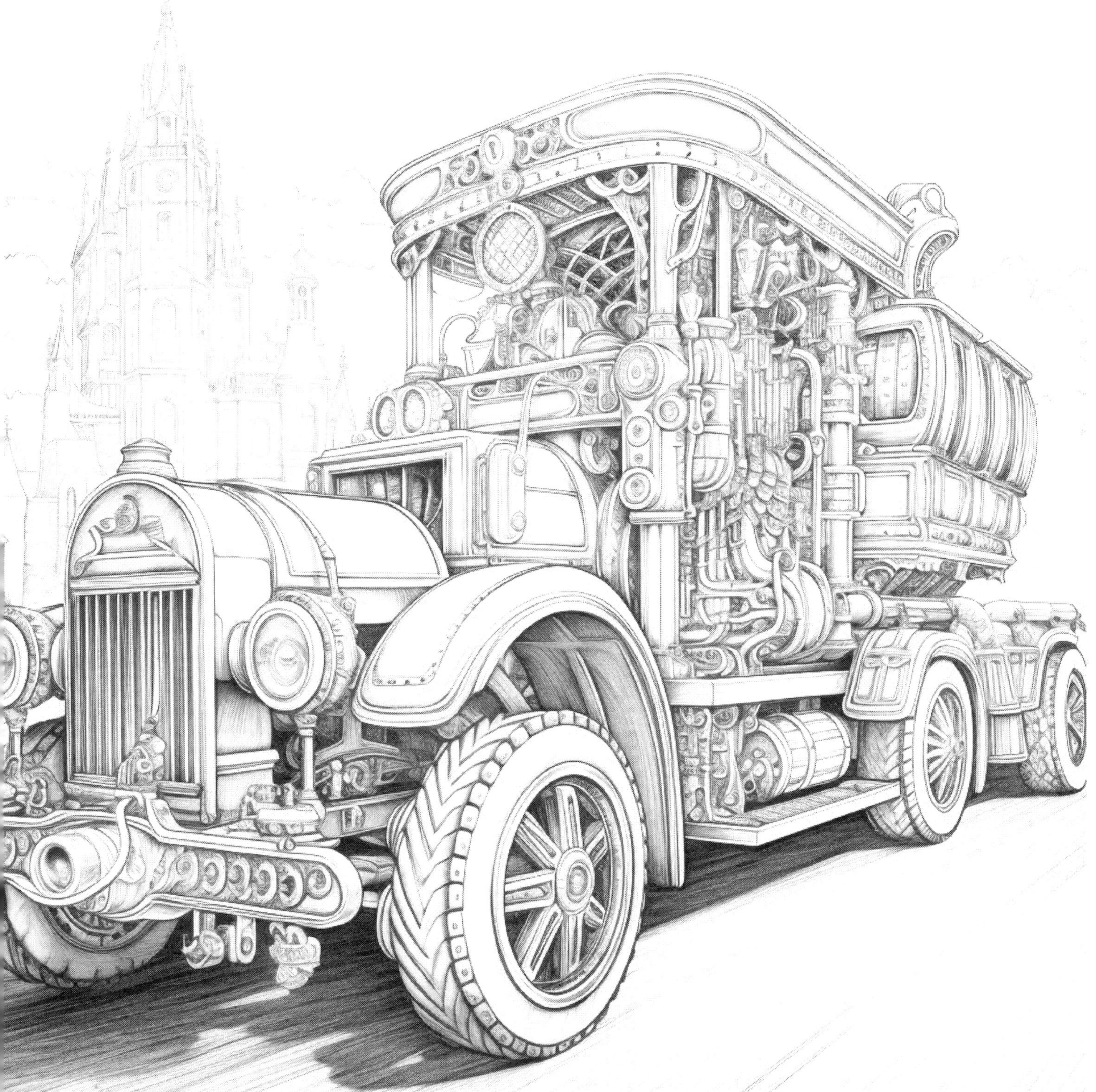

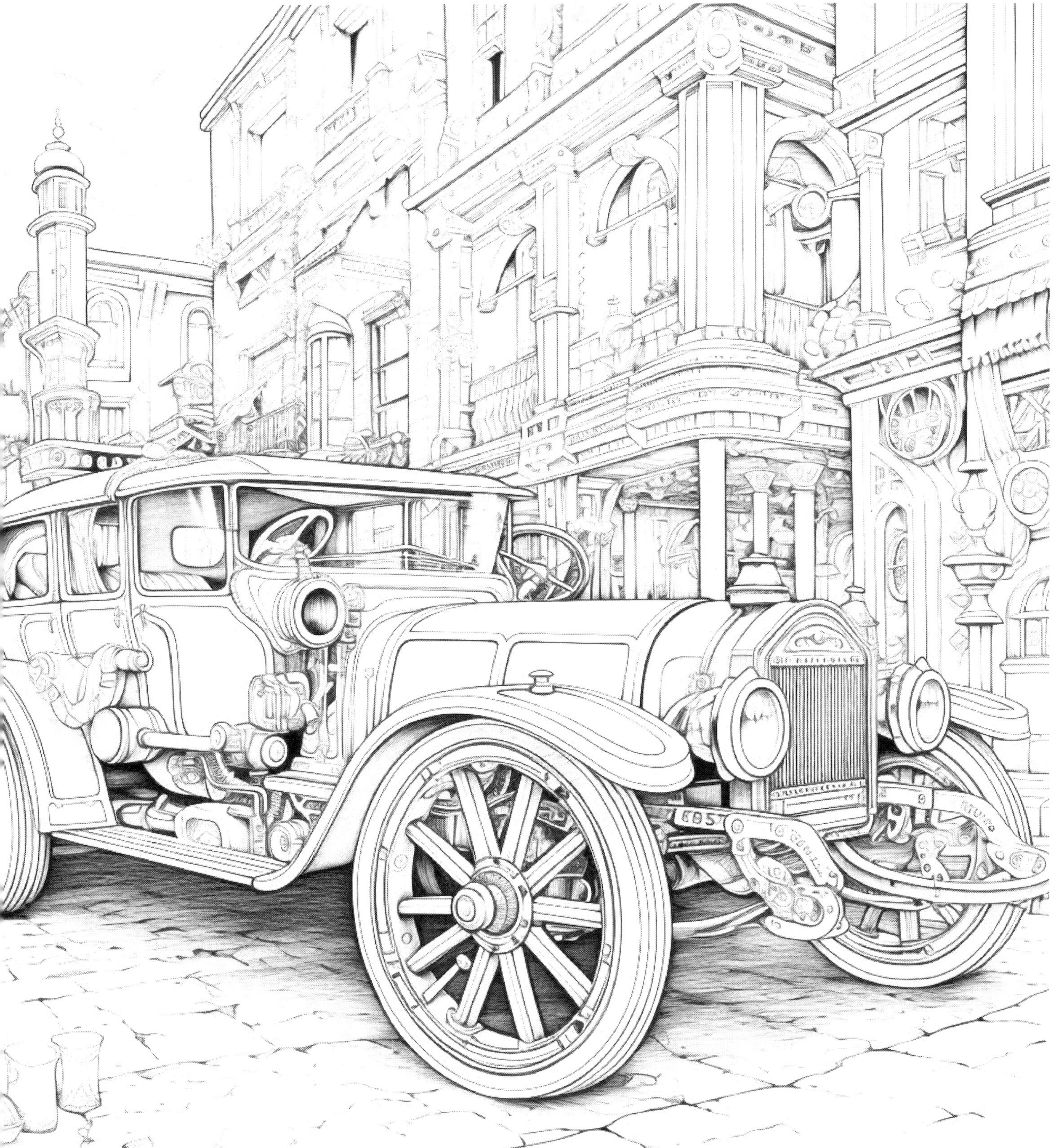

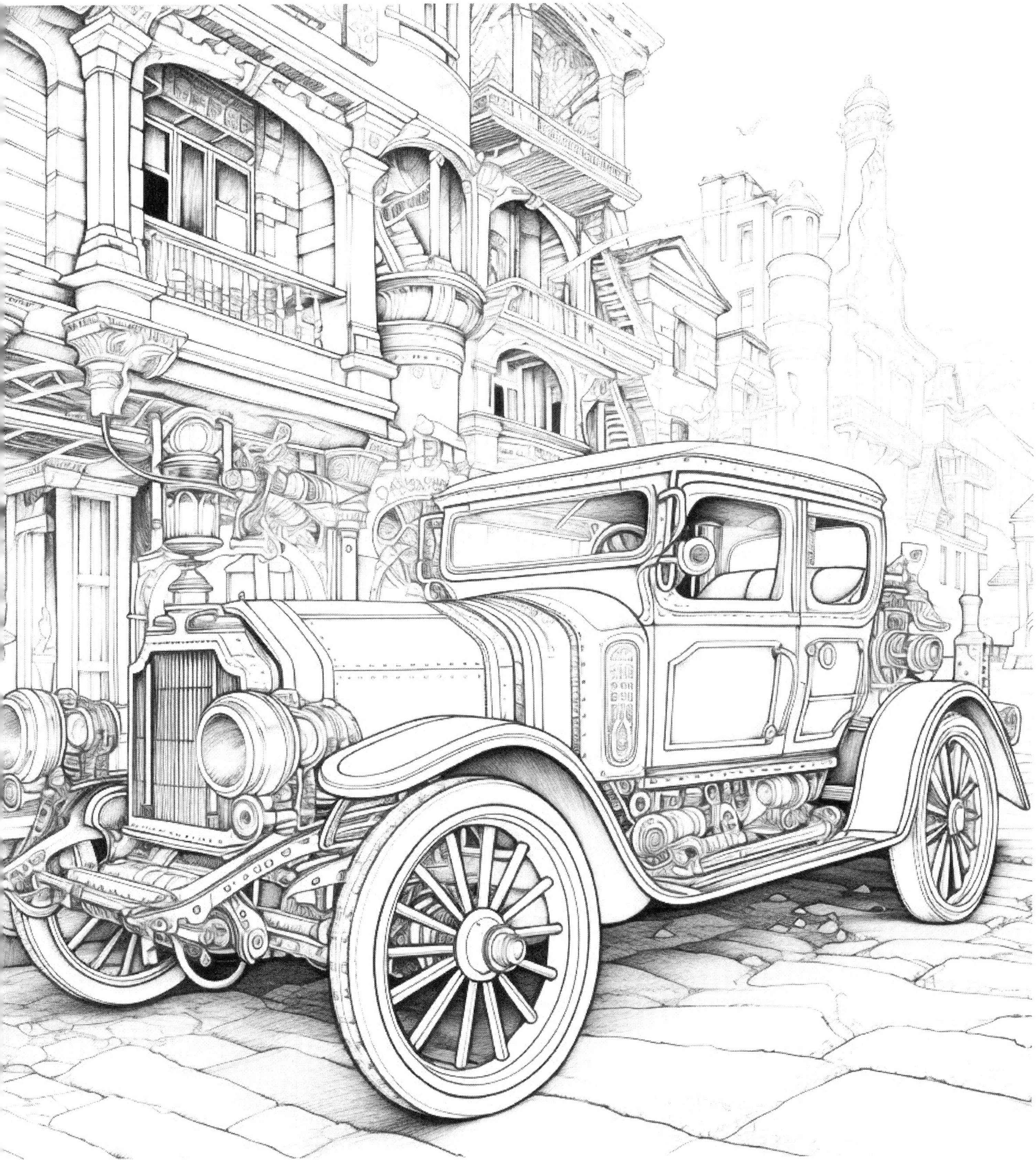

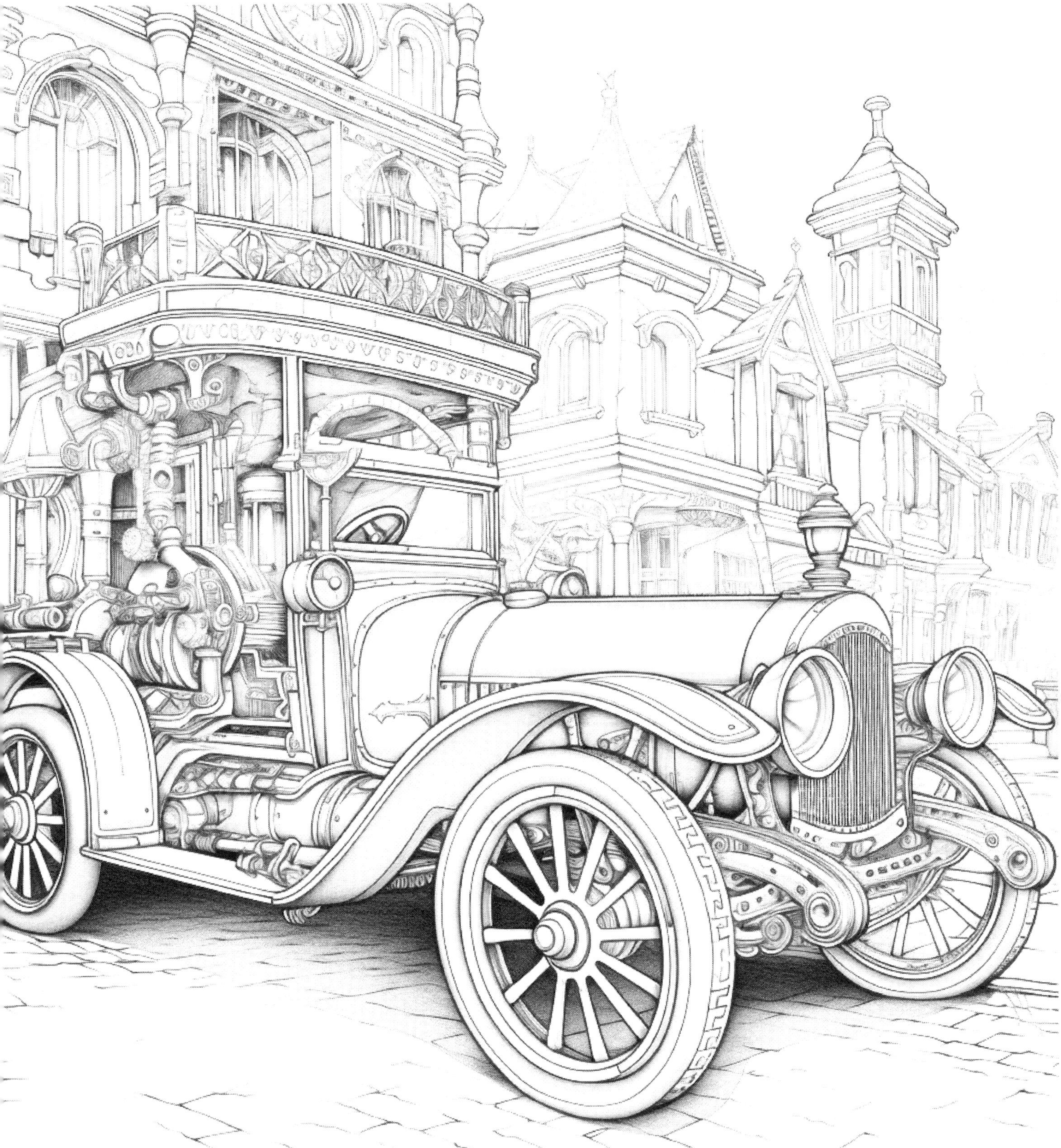

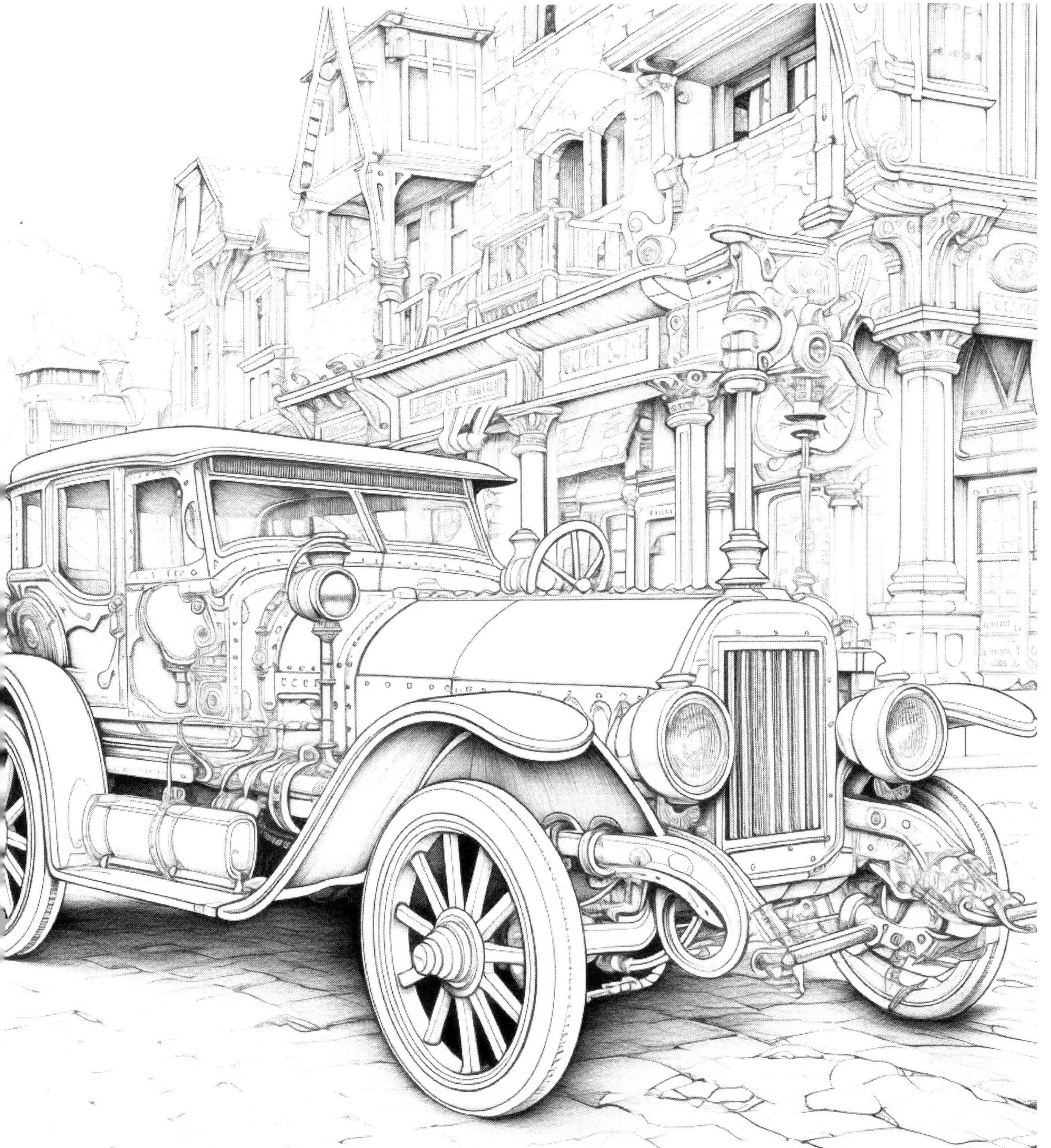

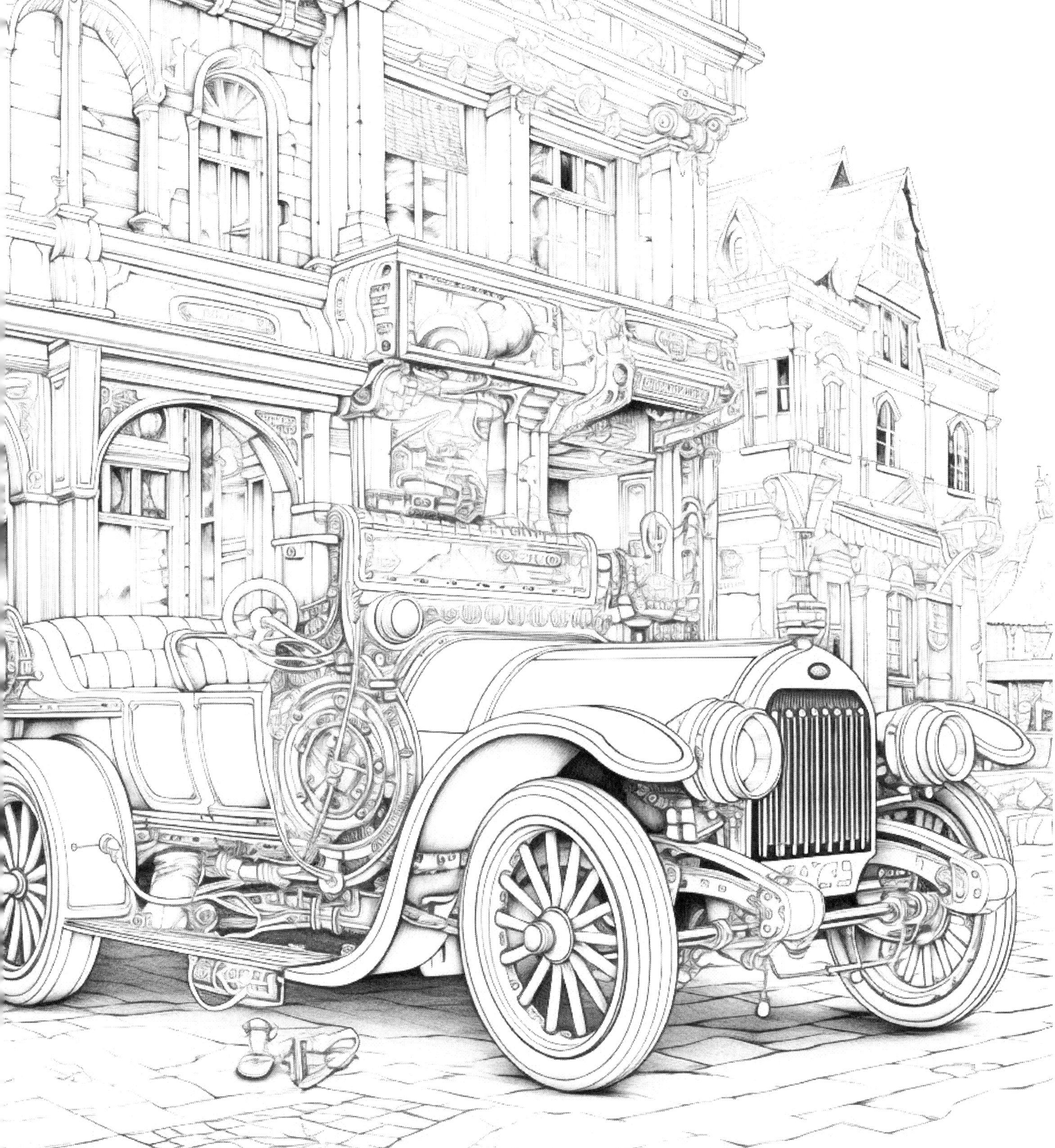

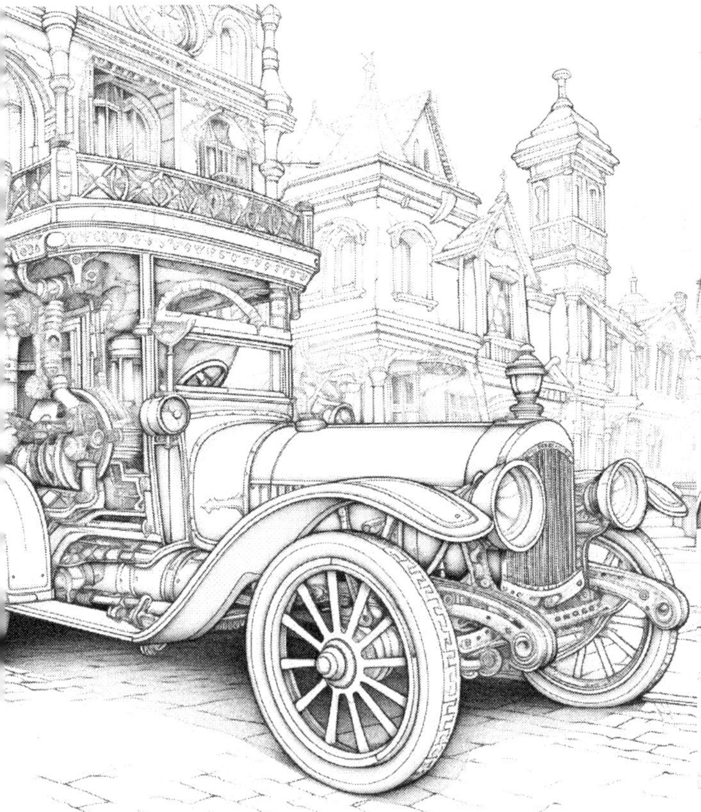

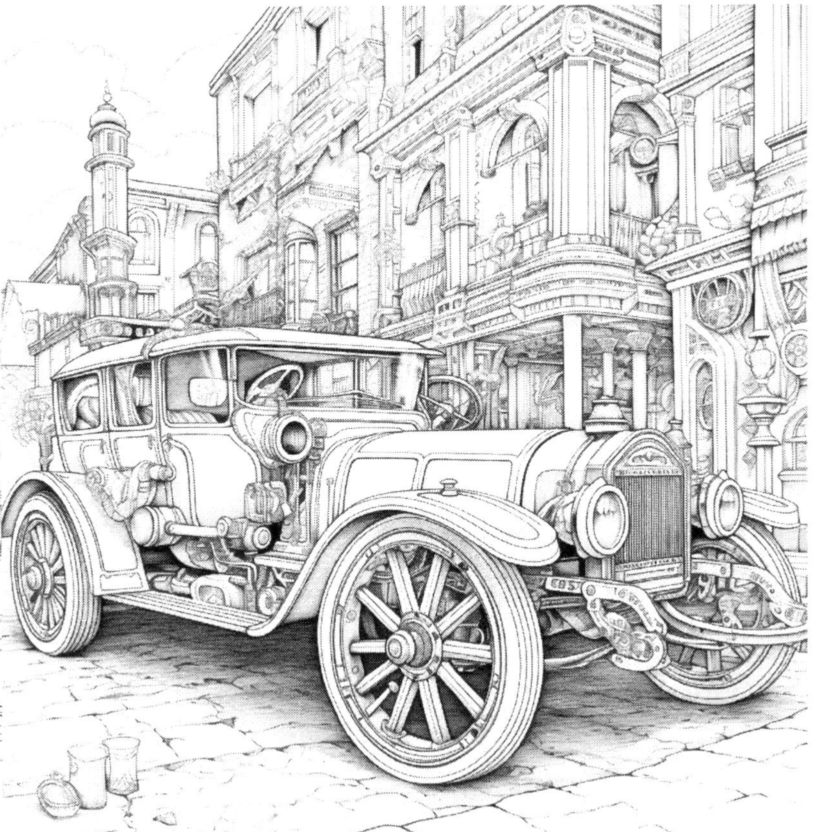

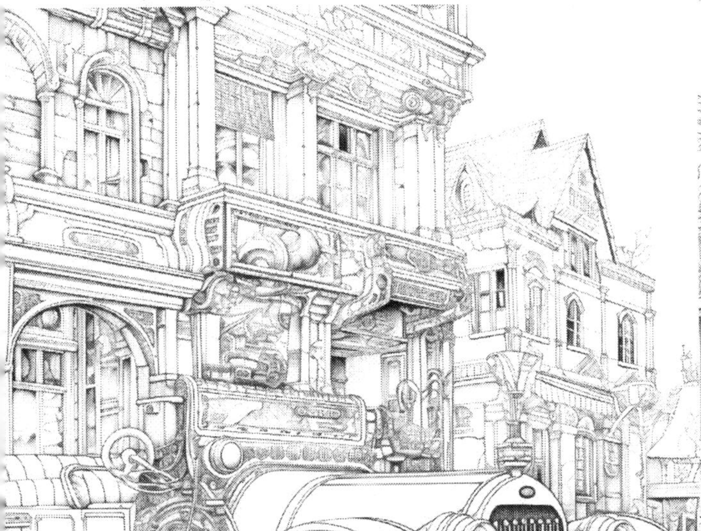

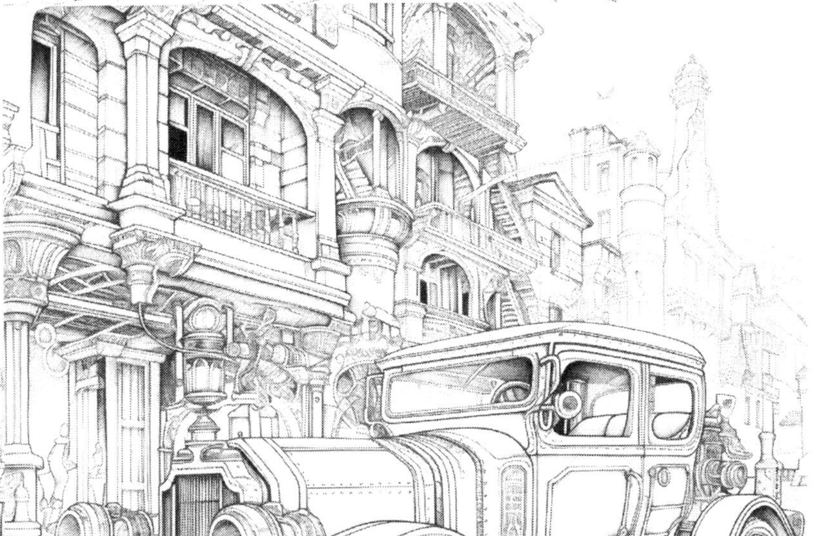

Printed in Great Britain
by Amazon

52083064R00029